you will feel whole again

parm k.c.

**THOUGHT
CATALOG**
Books

THOUGHTCATALOG.COM

THOUGHT CATALOG Books

Published by Thought Catalog Books, an imprint of Thought Catalog, a digital magazine owned and operated by The Thought & Expression Co. Inc., an independent media organization founded in 2010 and based in the United States of America. For stocking inquiries, contact stockists@shopcatalog.com.

Produced by Chris Lavergne and Noelle Beams
Art direction and design by KJ Parish
Creative editorial direction by Brianna Wiest
Circulation management by Isidoros Karamitopoulos

thoughtcatalog.com | shopcatalog.com

First Edition, Limited Edition Pressing
Printed in the United States of America

ISBN 978-1-949759-61-7

While you are awaiting the big things, the big wins, and the pure elation, please indulge in the small moments of joy. They aren't so small. They are the matter that make up something bigger. They are the ingredients for a life well lived, and days that end with a sigh of contentment. There is something so healing about taking pause to acknowledge when something small brings you a smile or a morsel of comfort. File these moments away. Keep a drawer in your mind where they live so you can pull from them as often as you need and remember that everything big is made up of a collection of the small.

Your healing belongs only to you. You are not healing for anyone other than yourself. Not to get someone back. Not to show someone what they're missing. Not to prove anything to anybody. You are healing for you. So you can finally feel some serenity in your life. So you free up room to savor everything this world has to offer. So you can be present in your own glory. You are healing to access the part of you that can love again, exist again, smile again. You are healing for you. So that you may never again give your best to someone who doesn't want good for you. So that you know better than to hand out love to every single person except yourself. You are healing so that the next time you walk through the dark, you will have faith that you'll catch the light again.

The beautiful thing about the emptiness left behind by those who walked away is that it will give you room to grow, expand, and breathe. You can fill it with whatever you like. You can choose what will move into that space and what replaces the things it used to house. You can leave it vacant for a time and teach yourself not to fear the hollow, but rather to embrace it. Take your time to fill it. Every single thing that falls into every single place of your life should be intentional.

There's no sense in me telling you that you'll be okay because right now, I know you won't believe me. You'll think I just don't know how you feel, or that I haven't been hurt as deeply as you have, or that I simply couldn't put myself in your shoes. None of this is true but I'm not here to convince you. So I'll tell you something else instead. I'll tell you that you'll make it through this day. Today. I'll tell you that if you take breath after breath, put one foot in front of the other, and move forward in even the tiniest way, that you will make it through this day. I'll tell you that when you go to bed tonight, you should feel proud of yourself for facing the day and facing yourself and mentally preparing yourself to do it all over again tomorrow. I'll tell you that if you try to make it through the day, each and every day, eventually it won't feel so arduous. Eventually both the morning and your heart won't feel so heavy. Eventually, you will feel whole again.

I've learned not to be so attached to any one version of myself. This is why I can let myself break so easily—I know I will rebuild something beautiful. I know there is no such thing as finding myself—that I am always right here within me. I know that love will change me, loss will change me, grief will change me. I don't fight these changes. I step into every new me and take along the remnants of my past self that are engraved on me but which don't define me. Everything I've been through is part of my unfolding, but none of it must *be* me if I don't desire it to be. I grasp that who I am is fluid and I don't owe the world the face they recognize. I only owe myself the vow to constantly unpeel my layers and let who I am just be. This is who I am.

I don't believe in "the one who got away." I believe that often, when we feel like we were left, hurt, or forsaken, we were really saved, spared, and protected. We view the people who are gone as "the one who got away" because we view relationships from a place of lack. We think someone leaving us means we are now missing something. We look at the distance between them and us and see sadness instead of opportunity. We see destitution instead of a new beginning. We cannot seem to shed true light on the relationship to reveal whether it added anything positive to our life, because we are too busy staring at the perceived void left behind. But people who leave you are not always "the one who got away." Sometimes they are the bullet you dodged.

A non-exhaustive list of reasons you should pursue healing: You never deserved the hurt in the first place. Your life could feel so free on the other side of healing. You are magic, and you deserve to feel as such. You cannot live in the dark forever—you must let some sun in. The world needs your heart. You have barely scratched the surface of who you could be. Happiness looks beautiful on you. None of us knows how much time we have, and it would be heartbreaking if we spent it in pain. You will feel the weight lift off your chest. Life doesn't have to be this heavy. You will attract into your sphere the people who deserve to be there. You will repel those who don't. You will sleep a little better. And wake up with more conviction. You'll feel like you can take deep breaths again. You will finally prioritize what matters to you. You can stop caring so much about what others think. You will protect your peace and wellbeing above all else. You will look back and be grateful. You deserve healing.

Seek a love that lets you love you too. A love that gives you room to be, just as you are. Seek a love that only grows the more you love yourself. One that isn't scared of your loyalty and devotion to you. You deserve a love that sees only benefits in your healing. And which cheers at the sight of you thriving. A love that knows your love for yourself doesn't take away your love for them. You should want for a love so self-assured that it does not feel threatened. One that doesn't ask you to hide or bury yourself. A love that reminds you to love yourself, even on the days you've forgotten how.

The further apart you grow from certain people, the closer you will grow to yourself. Pay attention to how close you feel to yourself when you're in the presence of others. Pay attention to if they are pulling you away from who you know you are at your core, and only loving you if you betray yourself. Always check in with your heart to see how you feel about yourself when you are around others. If you don't feel at peace, whole, and fulfilled, then they aren't the people you need in your life. If their love for you is conditional on you abandoning yourself, you are straying too far. There's something wondrous about the way we grow closer to ourselves the further away we move from these people. It will feel so much like finding the place you were always meant to be.

Treat yourself with gentleness, the way you wish others would. Set an example for yourself on how you deserve to be held. Let the way you regard yourself be the barometer and guideline for how others should regard you. The more you mistreat yourself, the more you desensitize yourself to abuse from others and are less likely to notice when they are hurting you. If only you could be softer with your own heart, you would finally see how others should handle it too. Hold yourself gently. The way you wish others would. Be the comfort that you crave.

We have been taught that we just need to hear some-one say the words "I love you" and have not been taught how important it is for us to genuinely feel it. The emphasis has always been placed squarely on the shoulders of the words. So, we don't know how to discern if someone really does love us. If they speak the words, we believe them. We're not taught to look at their actions. Or how they see us. We're not taught how to isolate the words and see if they move in unison with how the person treats us. There's so much more to love than words. There's how they hold you on your hard days. And how they celebrate you on the good ones. Look closely. Look at whether they pull you in or push you away. When you fall, do they laugh, or do they reach a hand to help you back up? If you stumble, do you feel a quiet confidence that they'll be there? Or are you looking around, wondering where they are in your darkest hours? It's action. Words are nice to hear. But it will always come down to action.

We forget that for some people, we are just warm bodies. And that some people have cold hearts. We forget that some people just need anybody next to them at night. That some people haven't learned to love themselves enough to be alone. That some people haven't learned to love themselves enough to search for someone who is what they truly want and instead are satisfied to simply fill the emptiness. They don't tell us we are simply filler, and so, in our desperation for love, we try to convince ourselves of a different truth. We tell ourselves they love us, we tell ourselves they need us, and we tell ourselves we need them too. You are so much more than a warm body.

It can be so difficult to accept someone leaving because slowly, over time, we handed over fragments of ourselves to them. A bit here and a bit there, and we don't even notice that there is not much left of us until they've departed and taken so much of us with them. Our devastation isn't so much about the fact that they're gone but about the fact that we didn't hold on to ourselves tightly enough. We recognize all the ways we gave up our dreams for them, hoping that if we gave them enough, they would stay. We told ourselves that by giving them so much, they would feel indebted to us and, just maybe, would remain by our side. We watched them walk away with what we falsely believe are the best parts of us, and it hurts. We're left feeling desolate and like we must recreate our identity from scratch. But they didn't get the best of us. The best elements of you are the ones that can never leave you. The ones that can't be taken. They're the ones you bring with you into every new experience, phase, and person you encounter. They are the essence of your soul and that which others can praise and love you for, but can never steal from you. You just can't see that they're still there because they are hidden under the mountain of hurt. Start peeling away the pain, and I promise you will uncover those pieces of yourself again.

It's funny how we can convince ourselves that someone who doesn't even like us, loves us. We stay with people who give us, at best, half the love we deserve, and we tell ourselves it's whole. We tell ourselves they make us whole. We create a whole relationship—an epic love story—without the other person even realizing or agreeing to it. They can treat us with contempt, and we tell ourselves they're just having a bad day. They pull away and we tell ourselves they just need some solitude. They put us last and we tell ourselves one day we'll come first. Our ability to tell ourselves the story we want to hear is so powerful and so impressive that I can't help but wonder why we don't tell ourselves a different story. I wonder why we don't tell ourselves that we deserve better. I wonder why we don't tell ourselves that we matter too. Why can't we tell ourselves that we shouldn't have to beg for love? If you can tell yourself someone loves you without confirmation from them, why don't you tell yourself that *you* love you and you won't accept less from others.

Potential is not a substitute for fulfillment. You cannot satisfy your heart with someone who could be what you need, but isn't. You will never be happy with a hologram of someone, rather than who they really are. It matters very little that you believe they can one day meet your needs, fill your heart, and lift you up. It matters much more whether they do meet your needs, fill your heart, and lift you up. Realize that you deserve to be with someone who is what you want–not someone who might be what you want in a different reality.

Let people be who they are. Let people do what they're going to do. Let them hurt you if that's what they choose, so you can accurately assess their place in your life. Let them leave you so you can fill that abyss with people who want to stay. Let them show you their true colors. Stop trying to control the outcome and convince them to act in the way you want them to. This doesn't allow you to see the true them. It doesn't allow you to determine if they align with you. You have to let people be themselves and make their own choices and *show* you who they are without intervention on your part. You cannot write a script for others on how to love you. You just have to let time and truth show you if they do.

Those who are offended by your self-love have a stake in you not loving yourself. You are so much easier to manipulate and mistreat when you don't like yourself. It's easier for others to walk all over you when you don't realize what you deserve and when you don't regard yourself highly. Those who are offended by your self-love know that it's harder for them to get their way with you. It's harder for them to speak to you unkindly, take advantage of you, and use you. They know you'll stick around if you don't see why you should leave. They can continue to hurt you. Put you down. Step on you to lift themselves higher. This is the only reason someone wouldn't want you to love yourself. Those who love you want you to love you too.

Maybe it's not that they cannot love you—maybe it's that they cannot even see the depths of your being. When someone doesn't love you, don't take this as an indicator of your lack of worth or a comment on what you deserve. It's very likely that this person simply can't *see* all that you are. This is not an invitation for you to try to help them see you. This is simply a reminder that for each person who cannot see and appreciate you, there will be someone out there who can.

If the success of your relationships, your friendships, your so-called love stories, is wholly dependent on you remaining small–please do not stay. If there is no room for you to spread out, blossom, and relax into yourself, you are not where you're meant to be. If they are only happy when you stay in the role they created for you, then you will never be happy.

When they leave and there is a speck of relief mixed into the sadness—that's when you know. Pay attention to this relieved feeling. Sometimes it can be so faint that it's easy to miss. Do you breathe slightly easier? Did you finally exhale? Do you feel a weight lifted off your chest? Look underneath the sadness. And the pain. And the grief. Look underneath the feeling of missing the one who is gone. Does some of the relief live under there? Does it feel like there's a ray of light folded away back there? This is the part of you that knows what you deserve. And that knows what you don't. This is the part of you that's been waiting for them to leave, or for you to leave, just so that you can finally see how bright your world can be without someone who hurts you.

It's funny how when our heart is broken, we think we can just will it to be unbroken. Like if we just tried harder or put forth more effort, we can somehow un-break it and heal ourselves. We would never do this with broken bones or broken objects–we would splint them, cast them, rebuild them, call in the experts. Yet we shame ourselves for our inability to fuse together shards of ourselves without doing the work and call-ing for help. I think this does a huge disservice to our hearts. We deserve to be cared for at a time when we feel broken. We deserve to be wrapped in warmth and support. We deserve to be mended.

Sometimes we stay in homes and with people who feel comfortable. The foundation could be crumbling, and the roof is leaking but still, we stay. We stay because we've been there for however long and we cannot fathom living elsewhere. All our belongings are there and to move them, to pack them up and decide which to keep and which to toss, feels too daunting. The comfort takes precedence over every possible reason we could have for leaving, because comfort is undoubtedly hard to come by. The length of time we've already stayed outweighs all other logic. Pain is like this too. We live in it for a time, burrow our way in and before we know it, we just cannot find the energy to make our way out. It's not pretty and it's not somewhere we want to invite anyone into, but it's comfortable. It becomes a veil that covers us in what seems like contentment but is really something else. It is really the thing that will keep us from arriving at where we're meant to go, and who we're meant to be. Don't live in pain forever simply because it resembles comfort. Take care to pack up your belongings. Take time to decide what to keep and what to toss. There is somewhere better for you to be.

It's rarely the big, "significant" memories that creep into the edges of our minds and leave us gutted. It's often the moments that we didn't even realize were tucked away in some corner of our heart that make their way to the forefront of our brains at the most inopportune of times. It's a seemingly insignificant Sunday morning walk through the park with them that flashes in our mind. It's the quick trips to the grocery store together to grab junk food for a quiet night in. It's falling asleep in front of the same movie you've seen a hundred times. These are the memories that seem to haunt you and prevent you from forgetting enough to move on. These are the moments that seem to have us in a chokehold, rendering us unable to break free even enough to envision all the beautiful moments that life still has in store for us.

The real you is under the trauma. Under the heartbreak. The real you is behind the grief and the tears that have been weighing you down. Who you are today—who you are in the midst of heartbreak—is not you. This is a you who has been forced to the forefront because of what you've gone through. This is a you who is a coping mechanism. Someone who is trying to learn. Heal. Grow. It's heavy to be this you, I know. It's exhausting and at the end of each day, you wish you could remove this front and rest into someone who is much more at peace. Remember, this is *not* you. The real you is beneath this person who is just trying to make it through each day. And they will come out. You will heal, gradually, and shed the pieces of this person who is just trying to survive. The real you will step out into the world and feel the breeze and the daylight again. It's just going to take some time.

We must remember that another person breaking us does not mean we have to break ourselves. We do not have to take the pain they've inflicted upon us and amplify it. We do not have to conclude that we deserve that pain, earned that pain, justify that pain. We can take that pain, affirm that it isn't ours to keep, understand that it is a reflection of *their* pain, set it down, and move forward.

What if you felt liberated every time someone walked away? The fact itself that they walked away is inherent proof they weren't for you. That is one less person in your life who should not have been there, and they are leaving of their own accord, without you having to ask them to go. They are saving you the work and the pain. Quietly thank them. Feel the liberation. And then keep going.

You will not always feel like you don't belong. There is a place in this world for you and there is a place in this life for you. No matter how much you feel like you shouldn't be here, you should. No matter how much you feel like you will never be wanted, you will. You won't feel lost and displaced forever. You will find the friends who are meant to bring you happiness. You will find the people who will love you the way you deserve. You will find love in yourself that is greater and brighter than anything you could have dreamed of. You will find the simple pleasures that remind you how good it feels to be here. And you will find the great big joys that make you feel alive. You are not here by accident. You belong here and I promise, you will find your place.

Every day cannot be a journey to healing. This is too much. It's too burdensome. Some days are just survival. Some days are about existing quietly. Many days are watching the clock tick until you can find some rest in the calm of the night. Every thought does not need to be so profound. There's too much already living in your mind for you to burden it with the constant pressure to heal.

You are not obligated to stay anywhere that you feel like a fraction of what you are. You don't need to stay anywhere where you don't feel loved. Treasured. Celebrated. You are allowed to walk away. You are allowed to walk away from people and situations that drain your energy, wear down your spirit, and leave you questioning your worth. You get to decide. You get to decide which people and places will be blessed with your presence. You get to decide who may feel your glow and who must live with your absence. You are not so firmly planted anywhere that you may not leave when you feel you don't belong there any longer.

I know you're tired of hearing that what doesn't kill you makes you stronger. What if for now, you don't want to be stronger? What if, for now, you just want to not see their face when you close your eyes? Or when you hear that one song, or when you sit on that particular park bench? What if instead of being stronger, you wish to simply make it through one day without quite so many tears, or quite so much regret? What if instead of strength, you'd just like the ability to not constantly refresh their social media, sift through the memory box for the millionth time, or replay that last conversation in your mind yet again? What if you want to feel like a person again—a person who never met them—because you didn't feel like this before you did. What if you'd like the permission to not necessarily be weak, but to just *feel* weak? At least for now, while it's all just so raw and fresh and the pressure of being "stronger" is just a little bit more than you can handle. What if you just want to feel what you feel now, and want to let the strength come later?

You are allowed to hurt, and you are allowed to let your hurt be seen. Pain is not meant to be concealed in the dark. You are not protecting others by hiding your hurt. You are only ensuring that you will walk the trail to healing alone. Pain is fed in the dark. It will only grow heavier the longer you keep it hidden. You can wear it on the outside. You can let the sun touch it and still be more than deserving of love.

Forgive yourself. Forgive yourself for the ways you've hurt yourself, and the ways you've let others hurt you too. Forgive yourself for not knowing better, not doing better, not being better. Forgive yourself for letting people who were wrong stay too long and take too much. Forgive yourself for not knowing how much love you deserved, how strong you can be, and what splendor you are. Forgive yourself for not seeking what should be yours because you didn't believe it could be yours. Forgive yourself for judging your tears, your pain, your grief. Forgive yourself for constantly going back to the ones who made your life darker and overlooking how much you truly are worth. Forgive yourself for putting everyone else above you and putting yourself last. Forgive yourself for not celebrating every form of yourself that was a stepping stone to who you are today.

Loneliness cannot be cured by other people. As long as you search for meaning and fulfillment and wholeness in other people, you will overlook how much of it lies within yourself. Loneliness will not subside when you find "the one" if you have not yet found calm within yourself, and if you have not yet made a home within yourself.

Sometimes the only way to let solace in is to let your-self break. If you cannot let yourself break, you delay the process. You delay the revolution. You delay the part where you get to emerge as a restored version of you. Breaking creates a pathway for something more. It allows everything you deserve to finally make its way into you. It allows you to get rid of all the hurt, the pain, and the toxicity that is trapped inside of you. Don't fear the breaking. Let yourself fracture and let the joy in.

The path to you can be isolating. It can be grueling and painful and it can hold a mirror up to your most difficult truths. The path to you can be undesirable, cold, and scary. It requires you to go alone and not rely on others for directions. It asks you to forget what you knew in the past and go forward with faith. It asks you to trust that you'll end up somewhere good, because wherever that is, you're meeting *you* there.

I've learned to value the rock bottom. Not at the time, of course. Certainly not while I'm living in the thick of it. But I've learned to see all the rock bottom stages as the pivotal points that launched me towards myself. I can look back and see how they set me on a trajectory towards action and towards rebuilding. I can clearly see how they forced me to take a magnifying glass to my life and to the people in it and evaluate where changes were desperately called for. Where major reform was needed, regardless of how painful. These have been the times that allowed me to break open just enough to see inside myself in a way I couldn't have otherwise–in a way that gives clarity to what parts inside of me require kindness and healing. I can take each of my victories and trace backwards to the rock bottom that led me there.

One of the most impactful things we can do to move forward is to accept who people are and stop rewriting their personalities. Stop rewriting their intentions. Stop rewriting their hearts. We tend to have such difficulty accepting that someone doesn't belong in our life and that they may be the cause of our pain because we lie to ourselves about the effect they have on us. Our optimism pushes us to believe the best in them at the expense of our own wellbeing. We know that acknowledging who they are will be the first step in letting them go and that is scary. So we hang on. To who we wish they were, to how we wish they made us feel, and to what we thought they were before we knew them better. We delay the pain of the goodbye. And when we delay it, we compound it. It's time to stop rewriting people and simply read them as they are.

You are going to meet people who don't want you to recognize your own light. They want to benefit from your light without you seeing it so that they don't have to compensate you for it. They want to use it to light their way. They depend on you not comprehending it. They depend on you being so unaware of it that you give it away for free. They believe that if you never realize its power, they can continue to gain from it without ever really giving you anything in return for it. So please, see it. See your own light. Revel in it and let it guide your way. And share it only with those who not only truly deserve it, but who help you see it too.

This is how you let go of people who don't love you:
you love yourself.

Your past is not your past if you are still living there. If you cannot let go, if you cannot step outside of who you were when you were there, you haven't moved on. You are not living in the present if you have one foot planted in all that has gone by. To remember is one thing. To ruminate in what could have been, or what you believe should have been, is another. Your past will never be your past if you cannot stop looking back. Looking back is living in a ghost town. You can see it all so clearly, but do not have the power to touch any of it. And so, you become a ghost. Your past is not your past if you are haunted by it, and if you are haunting it. Let it be a part of your existence, but do not let it be your whole existence.

Let go of your attachment to the old you. Appreciate that you are not defined by who you used to be, what you used to think, and how others used to perceive you. Within our lifetime, we are a thousand different people. We are constantly evolving and who you are today may have nothing in common with your past self. If you cling to old pieces of yourself, you will never reach the potential of who you're meant to be. That frozen feeling that so many of us have—the one whose root cause is so hard to identify—it comes from the grip we have on our past. You must grieve and then let go of your past self to step into what's meant for you.

Each heartbreak will change you. This is a gift. You were never meant to stay the same. You are not meant to reach the end of your life and resemble the person you were at the beginning. Every time you think you have been crushed, you are being ground into a newly strengthened you. The way heartbreak touches you, the way it colors you and moves you and alters the very essence of you, is a part of your fabric. It's all leading you towards yourself and it's all teaching you how heavily you will always be able to rely on you. Watching yourself grow from hurt and pain and not only recover, but flourish will leave you with an unshakable faith in yourself.

I want you to know that you are so much more than the sadness you feel, and the parts of you that you think you hate, and the regrets you can't let go of. You are more than the people who have hurt you, the people who have left you, and the people who never even bothered to show up. You are more than the perceived mistakes you've made, and more than the dreams you haven't yet chased.

What if I told you that you are not alone in feeling so hopeless? That the darkest thoughts that occupy your mind—others have them too? What if I told you that your heaviest emotions are not the cause of your loneliness but are what actually connect you to the rest of humanity? Our most difficult feelings are what we all have in common. We have more community than we know, yet we feel an immense and crushing sense of seclusion. Our unspoken grief, if spoken, would resonate with so many. Put your pain into words, not only so that you may heal but so that you may unveil the inevitable support that is awaiting you.

Consider this. It's not that you need to learn more about love, but that you need to unlearn what you thought you knew about love. So many of our ideas about love were formed in the years when we hadn't experienced it yet. We looked to Disney movies, romantic comedies, and fiction. We thought love was someone sweeping you off your feet and you being there for them unconditionally, no matter how they treat you. We thought love would save us and be the answer to every question. Real love is none of these things and can only truly be learned through experience and time.

When someone hurts you, it can be so tempting to believe you deserved it. It can be so tempting to fall into the pattern of self-blame and pity. I challenge you to try something different—don't try to find the meaning. Don't try to find the "why." Let it rest. It is likely not about you, and entirely about them. We cannot begin to fathom the dimensions that exist within each person, and each of these is a factor in their actions. Sometimes you are simply a bystander of someone else's anger and unhealed pain. This doesn't make it okay, and it doesn't make it fair. But knowing this prevents you from internalizing their toxicity and letting it marinate in your heart. Knowing this allows you to let their hurt slide off you and onto the ground where it belongs.

I know it kills you that you will probably never get an apology from them. So I will be the one to apologize to you. I'm sorry that you let the wrong one in. I'm sorry they didn't see how precious your heart is. I'm sorry that you feel deceived by who they pretended to be. I'm sorry that you now question yourself when you're simply someone who wants to give others a chance. I'm sorry they didn't hear your voice. I'm sorry you feel embarrassed and ashamed. I'm sorry that you're scared of what the future holds for you. I'm sorry people lie. I'm sorry someone preyed on your vulnerabilities. I'm sorry they tainted the concept of love for you. I'm sorry they didn't respect your boundaries. I'm sorry you didn't respect your boundaries. I'm sorry you kept quiet to keep the peace. I'm sorry you had to beg for the bare minimum. I'm sorry you never came first. I'm sorry you feel used. I'm sorry for all of it.

There is no shame in seeking help. There is no shame in admitting to yourself and others that you simply cannot carry everything you have to carry all on your own. There is no shame in asking others to step in and lighten your load. We were put on this earth alongside other souls so that we can be of service to each other. As strong as you are, you were not meant to suffer alone, and you cannot hold everything on your back without it breaking. There is no shame in the cry for help.

Sometimes when I feel like I am buried under the pain, I remind myself that the world is big and I am small. And though you might think this does not provide re-lief, it most certainly does. If the world is big, there are so many others. Others who share my pain and know my ache. And if I am small, and there are so many oth-ers, then I can be dug out of the hurt.

You are grieving not just because they're gone, but because you discarded your own voice and your needs to keep them around all this time. You are struggling to identify who you've come to be and you're ashamed that you hid all of the traits that make you *you* in order to feel worthy of their love. You were scared to let them see the real you because the edited you is the only one they seemed to approve of. This truth is harder to swallow than the leaving itself. You know the work it will take to unearth the parts of you that you've kept undercover for so long and that's a daunting task. It's daunting but you can do it. You can find your way back to that person, the person you were before you locked them up in the pursuit of acceptance. Make it your purpose from this day forward to find that person and never let them go.

You know exactly what you deserve. You are not confused. You are just struggling to acknowledge what you deserve because once you do, you will have to let go of so many people and things in your life that do not align with that. And you're not ready to do this. You're not ready to say goodbye. So, you tell yourself that you're unsure. Unsure of what you need, want, and desire. Unsure of what you are entitled to. You delay these endings because you anticipate the pain they will bring. In doing so, you are also delaying the bliss you will feel when you finally act in accordance with what you know you deserve.

Closure is a fallacy. It's a farce we invented to excuse the yearning we have to stay close to those who hurt us. It's what prevents us from moving forward. It's an illusion that tells us we cannot leave the room until someone else opens the door for us and gives us permission to step through it. It holds you back and holds you down. Keeps you stuck. Keeps your feet firmly planted in that which does not let you grow, shine, or thrive. To say goodbye without closure takes strength but it also takes wisdom. It requires the knowledge that you aren't missing anything by moving on without closure. The best closure you will ever receive is the relief you will feel when you simply walk away from the pain and don't look back.

You are allowed to be upset when someone hurts you. You are not obligated to always be the "bigger person" and invalidate your own feelings. There is no need to immediately search for the lesson in the hurt, or instantly thank the one who hurt you for gifting you resiliency. You are allowed to just feel betrayed and wounded. You don't have to ingest the pain. You don't have to let it simmer inside you, only to bubble up when you least expect it. The feelings of those who hurt you are not more important than your own. You don't owe them forgiveness. You don't owe them understanding. You owe yourself all of that. You owe yourself the freedom to honor your feelings, however heavy they may be.

Sometimes your love for them and your love for you cannot live together in harmony. And for so long, you will sacrifice your love for you so that you may keep on loving them. You know deep down that there is not enough space to hold both, and so, you choose them. But eventually you must choose yourself. Eventually you must realize that if you are loving someone who takes all of your love, and leaves none for you, you will run out. You will run empty. And this is no way to live.

Some people don't love you. They love what you can do for them and how you make *them* feel. And this is precisely why not everything you lose is a true loss. Even though it may not feel like it right now, losing these people will be one of the biggest gains of your life. It will allow you to stop wasting your love, energy, and devotion on someone who is only in it for themselves with no regard for what they give back to you. A relationship with no reciprocity is hardly a relationship at all.

Single is not the worst thing you can be. Unhappily attached, subject to constant criticism, tolerating mistreatment. These are all far less desirable. The problem is we've been fed a narrative that if you're not coupled up, you're doing something wrong. We've been taught that if you are by yourself, this means you haven't been chosen. And a lack of being chosen is inherently viewed as the lowest point a person can reach. The message is that you're doing life wrong. That you can't enjoy what life has to offer because doing so in your own company just isn't enough. *That your own company isn't enough.* But I repeat, being single is not the worst thing you can be. There are couples who are faking it for an audience, yielding to societal pressure, and staying together because they're just so scared that being single is the worst thing you can be. And there are people who are walking through life by their own side. Steeping in pure happiness. And knowing that they are not truly alone.

Bravery is letting yourself break. Bravery is having faith that you will get up again. It is conviction in yourself and your ability to heal. Bravery is not the fake smile meant to convince the world you're fine when you're not. Bravery is letting yourself fall to show others it's okay for them to fall too. Bravery is holding your heart in the palm of your hand and vowing to treat it graciously. Vowing to never hand it to anyone who won't treat it with empathy. Bravery is withholding judgment of your tears and the heaviness and the days in bed. Bravery is reaching out for help when you can't move on from the tears and the heaviness and the days in bed. Bravery is letting the right one peer inside you to see the injured parts, the dark parts, the wilted parts, and leaning into their soft touch.

It's not enough to learn the lessons. You must put them into daily action. Every experience that tests us teaches us something. But if we do nothing with those lessons —if we change nothing about ourselves and our lives— we're wasting them. The lessons are the most valuable gifts we will receive in our lifetime, but they are not meant to be locked away in a safe like jewels. They are meant to be used.

I know that if you pictured the person you want to be with—the qualities they have, what they add to your life, and what they subtract from your life—it wouldn't truly be the person you're missing. You may protest and insist they are the one you want, but you must stop and take these words to heart. If you could create the person your heart wants, it's not them. It's not their treatment of you. It's not the way they left you feeling. You've just convinced yourself it is by making allowances for their behavior. And forcing puzzle pieces into places they don't belong. The end result doesn't look how you wanted but it's close enough for you to turn a blind eye and placate yourself. Choose to be honest with yourself instead. I know that if you pictured the person you want to be with, if you pictured the very *soul* of that person, it would not be the person that you are missing.

There will be people who don't want to grow and who don't want you to grow either. Let them stay where they are. Progress anyway. Don't accept anybody's invitation for you to remain static with them. They are on their own journey and simply may not be ready for growth. You are. You are ready. You have been ready. You are ready to grow into who you were always meant to be. And you can only do so if you are standing beside those who support your evolution and want to see you bloom into the highest you.

You will not receive reparation from the one who hurt you. Let go of the need for this—it won't help you anyway. It will not help you forget the past or forget the hurt. Turn your focus to *you*. Seek closure with yourself. Repair your relationship with you. Don't let what happened be a distraction from the fact that you need to hold yourself, comfort yourself, show mercy to yourself. Turn inwards for the ability to become free. I swear, it exists in you. Right now, you can't see that because you're so focused on receiving some type of grace from them that they've never even displayed before. This isn't where recovery lies. It lies beside you, around you, in your own being. You get to decide where you go from here and you get to decide which configuration of you is taken into the future. Sit with yourself and ensure you are tending to your own heart in a way nobody else ever will. Peace lives here. In the work you do on yourself.

You can save yourself so much pain by listening to your inner voice. You are not unclear. You are not unaware. You are not unsure. You're just not listening to yourself. You're listening to everyone around you and prioritizing their wants, their needs, their projections of you. You must silence all the noise and check in with yourself. Be your own trusted advisor. Nobody else has ever lived inside your head, your body, your mind, your experiences. They cannot see what you see and they cannot feel what you feel. Even the ones who know you best don't truly *know* you. You know you. So take a deep breath. Quiet the noise. And ask yourself for the answers. They exist within you. Everything you need exists within you.

What if you just gave into it? To the feeling of your heart breaking. Not just in a fleeting puppy love kind of way but in an, 'oh my God I think my heart is actually physically breaking,' kind of way. What if you said to yourself, my heart is breaking today, and it will be breaking tomorrow, but perhaps one day, it won't be. What if you just sat with that, and took a breath in, and then a breath out, and let whatever feeling you feel just be. Let those feelings sit within you. Would it cure you immediately? Probably not. But you don't need curing. That's not what you're missing. What you're missing is self-compassion. And the ability to let today be what it is. And an understanding that *feeling* broken is different than *being* broken. Feelings are not forever. Let them wash over you and then let them pass through, however long it takes.

The people who belong with you, who are right for you, and meant for you, won't make you feel shame. They won't make you feel unimportant, and they won't make you feel lost. They won't make you question your worth, nor will they make you believe you don't matter. They will never leave you confused, and they will never ask you to abandon yourself. They won't diminish you. They won't ridicule you. They won't feel so heavy. They won't leave you in pieces, and they won't steal your peace. The things and people that are right for you won't feel so wrong. They will lift you up and make you feel at home within your own body and within their presence. The things and people that are right for you will just *feel* right for you.

You don't need to be grateful for your trauma. You don't need to give it thanks for making you who you are. If you are angered by it, if you wish it had never happened, if you view it as your darkest time, you are not alone. You don't have to feel that what didn't kill you made you stronger. You are stronger because of what you are made of, and the people and situations that have hurt you do not deserve any of the credit. You do not need to view your pain with toxic positivity in order to move on from it.

What if you just did it? What if you left the person who mistreats you. Or wrote the book. Or took the class. What if you called the therapist. Made an appointment. What if you booked that trip. That one you've been wanting to take forever. Took your first step towards healing. What if you told them how you feel. Mustered up the courage to inch yourself closer to the real you. What if you just went for it? What if you reached out to that friend. The one who needs you and whom you need just as much. What if you made a list of what you want in your life and what you don't, and finally started acting in synchronicity with that? What if you started being honest with yourself about the parts of your life that are dragging you down. Stealing your faith. Damaging your psyche. What if you let go? Of everything and everyone that has been holding you back from being who you want to be—who you know you really are deep down inside.

Your purpose isn't to convince anyone to love you. Or to show them what you're worth. Your purpose is to be as pure and authentic as you can be. This means honoring your passions. Acknowledging your flaws. Seeing your own worth. Upholding your boundaries. In doing this you might lose people. And this sounds incredibly scary right now, but look beyond the initial fear. The best thing we can do is be so unapologetically ourselves that we *do* end up pushing away those not meant for us. After the initial loneliness, something amazing starts to happen. In time, you will start to relish in your own presence. The quiet days without them will turn into treasured days with yourself. The chasm you once wished they'd fill will now be a safe haven for you to uncoil into. Loneliness will turn into tranquility. And then, like a magnet, you will draw into your life the people who deserve this season of you.

You don't need other people to see your worthiness in order for you to see it. You don't need to wait for someone else to tell you you're beautiful before you're allowed to believe you're beautiful. You don't need anyone to love you before you recognize that you are lovable. You don't need anyone to claim you in order for you to comprehend how much you have to offer. You don't need anyone to call out your brilliance, or your pure heart, or the way you leave a trail of light behind you, in order for you to be that light.

While you are healing, I hope you still take care of yourself. I hope you go to bed on time, tucking yourself delicately into clean sheets. I hope you find the strength to shower and let warm water wash away the pain of the day and maybe even some of the years spent letting them make you feel unlovable. I hope you feed yourself well and nourish your soul too. I hope you spend time with the people who love you, because I promise they still exist. I hope you read moving stories, filled with love and pain and growth to remind you that yours is a story just like that and really, you aren't alone. I hope you soak up art and sunshine, and soak up the luxury of your own unapparelled company. While you are healing, I hope the parts of you that you kept hidden in an attempt to keep someone around start making their way to your surface again. I hope the words you suppressed and stifled and consumed will spill out messily onto pages and into songs. I hope you pick up every hobby you had put down, all the instruments and paintbrushes and pens and turn them into music and art and poems that are so exceptionally *you* that you'll have no choice but to finally acknowledge your strength, take a deep breath, and say "I'm going to be okay."

You deserve to receive all that you give. You deserve someone who returns to you all of the magic that you pour into them. You deserve to feel like the radiance you shine onto others also makes its way back to you, warms your skin, and stays in your heart. You deserve to be met halfway and to feel like you are not giving endlessly without being replenished. You deserve reciprocity. You deserve to be treated with all of the kindness that you carefully bestow onto the ones you care for. You deserve to feel cared for too. You deserve to feel like the ones you provide a resting place for will also let you rest within them. You deserve to be treated lovingly and with ease, just like you do for those around you. You deserve to enjoy the fruits of the seeds you have so lovingly and tenderly planted.

The next time you are punishing yourself for a relationship not working out, I want you to ask yourself where you got the idea that you had to get love right on the first try. Or the second. Or the third. With most things in life, we are so aware that progress takes practice, introspection, and reflection. But when it comes to love, we seem to think we'll instantly know exactly what we want, what we're searching for, and what to do when we think we've found it. We seem to think we can succeed without moving through the experience. A relationship with another human being with their own set of baggage, flaws, and trauma—just like we all have—is not something most of us will perfect at first attempt. So, stop rushing, remove yourself from the race, and take your sweet time figuring it out.

There's a reality possible for you where you are healed. Where you finally see yourself, your own brilliance, your strengths, and everything you bring to you and those around you. There's a reality where you no longer hang on to the words of those who hurt you and the actions of those who left you wounded. There's a reality where you've let go of the pain and embraced healing. There's a world where so much growth has occurred inside of you that you barely remember the person you used to be, yet still have empathy towards them because you know they helped get you there. There's a reality where you easily choose yourself, and where you no longer see yourself through the eyes of those that have rejected you. It exists on this plane, in this universe, and within your lifetime. But it requires you to let go of so much. It requires you to let go of believing what other people tell you about yourself, rather than listening to what you know of you to be true. It requires you to put down all the pieces of the past you've been holding onto, and to stop nurturing dead connections. It requires you to become better at walking away from things and people who don't fill your soul with rapture and who don't bring you closer to who you want to be.

As important as messages of self-love, independence, and knowing your worth are, I also believe we must acknowledge the toll that heartbreak can have on you. I think we need to give grace to those going through it and feeling crushed under the weight of it. Those who aren't in a place in their healing yet where they can foresee how much lighter they'll feel one day. We need to understand that saying goodbye to someone you imagined living your days out with can knock over the strongest of us. Rewriting a future that you thought was a sure thing is not light on the heart. I think we need to go easy on ourselves if we just can't seem to get back up like we thought we would. Heartbreak is no insignificant thing.

Please stop putting people up on a pedestal. Stop believing that you are lucky to have even a second of their time and affection. Stop convincing yourself that they are the best you can do. Stop convincing yourself that this is the best you can be. Please take care to evaluate who you allow into your life, heart, and circle. Stop accepting crumbs of attention when you know you deserve so much more. Stop making decisions about who you love from a mindset of scarcity, fear, or desperation. Please see that you can have more. More love, more warmth, more respect. Take a harder look at how they treat you, speak to you, view you. Please stop putting people up on a pedestal for if you do, you will only ever view others as above you, and you will never see how tall you truly stand.

If you spent so long being what they wanted you to be, or what you thought they wanted you to be, the silver lining is that now that they are gone, you finally get to be *you*. You're free now. And even if you don't know who that is yet, you get to take your time creating a form of yourself that only you get the final say on. After so long shrinking and rearranging yourself to fit into the box they wanted you in, you can take yourself out of the box, break down your essence, and decide if the being you see in the mirror is truly reflective of you. You are not just becoming you. You are creating you.

People can choose who they'd like to be. Stop thinking that you can make the choice for them. If they choose to be someone who mistreats you, that is on their conscience—not yours. We do not have enough influence over others to ensure they will love us and treat us well. And none of us should have this much influence over another being. What we do have influence over however, is how we choose to respond. And who we allow into our personal universe. We have the choice to draw a line that we do not permit others to cross. And we have the choice to bid farewell to those who do.

There is more to you than this pain. And there is more to life than the person who caused it. You don't exist for anyone else. You don't exist as merely a tiny part of the memoir of the one who hurt you. You have your own memoir. You are the protagonist in a much bigger tale that can only play out if you trust that you are so much more than the pain, and that your life is so much more than the person who inflicted it.

It's okay if you lost yourself in someone else and are still fighting to find your way out. It's normal for the wounds to take time to heal. And for you to slowly move on. To rebuild. To find your way out of them and back to you. It is too heavy a burden to carry someone so deep in your being, to love them, to have them be a *part* of you and then walk away unscathed. So take your time. Treat your healing like a ritual. Go through the motions, even if you know you are only going through the motions. Let yourself feel lost. Let yourself feel like you won't be found again. It's not true, but fall into this feeling anyway. Let your healing be intentional. Let the wounds turn to scars slowly and with purpose. Let each night feel heavy and each morning empty. Until it doesn't anymore.

Some people will prefer the version of you who never transforms. They will love you as long as you fit into the mold they've created for you in their mind. You will never be diluted enough for these people. And you will lose yourself trying to be. You can fold yourself up into pieces so tiny you cannot see yourself anymore, and still, you will be too big for them. These are not the people who belong on your journey with you. You belong with people who will rejoice in your unfolding and want you to take up space.

There are some people who will try to paint over you. They will try to paint over who you truly are and paint you into what they need. They will project their desires all over you, using a myriad of deceivingly beautiful colors so that you too will be convinced that this is what you are. They will gaze adoringly at what they created, and you will bask in the way they love their art, so much so that you take this representation of you as truth. You will pray these colors never wash away so that you don't lose their love. Even if you don't feel it's you. However, there is another way. You don't have to accept what is projected onto you. You can grab hold of the paintbrush and decide for yourself what you will be. You can choose the colors, the pattern, the vision that you wish. You can present yourself to the world as you really are. And the people who appreciate the art that you are, the works that you created *yourself*—those are the ones whose love will feel pure.

If today you feel unwanted, you need your own heart more than ever. The days we feel abandoned are the days that call for our most gentle selves. They are the days that need us to hold ourselves tightly, speak to ourselves kindly, and be the warmth in which to land. These are the days that call for our forgiveness. Our humanity. Our tenderness. The days we feel lonely are the days we must be a merciful companion to ourselves. We must remind ourselves that there is a caring human who will always show up for us. Love us. See us. These are not the days to speak to ourselves harshly, cut ourselves with words, punish ourselves. If you are lonely, you need to show up for yourself. If you are lonely, you need everything you have inside of you to bubble up to the surface and be the balm for what ails you.

You are not the sum of your heartbreaks. You are not a quilt sewn together from pieces of the people who have hurt you. You are not traces of the ones who left, nor shards of what has cut you. Your heartbreaks have happened to you, but they are not *you*. You are something else. You are the summation of every time you have risen. You are the totality of each and every time you have chosen to take a step up and a step forward after falling. You are the climb. You are the conquest over what you have left behind and faith in what you know lies ahead.

The next time you find yourself begging someone to stay, remember that people who want to stay, stay. People who want to go, go. You are not able to make anyone do what you want them to do—you don't have this power over others. Convincing yourself that you do is only a recipe for heartbreak. You will believe you are doing something wrong because you're unable to make them bend to your will, when really, you don't even have that ability. You aren't doing anything wrong. Let people decide for themselves where they want to be, and where they do not. Know that if they do choose to leave, it wasn't your fault, and you will heal. And you will only be closer to finding the ones who want to stay.

There is a difference between a person and their promises. People are not their promises. People are not what they say they will do. Or how they say they will treat you. Or who they vow to be. People are the lived actions they carry out day after day. A person's true character lives at the intersection of their promises and their actions. Do not be so hungry for affection that you fill up on promises alone. You deserve more than just promises whose fruition will never see the light of day.

I've learned the most about love from those that did not truly love me. I've learned what it doesn't look like and how it shouldn't feel. I've learned that it's easy to say "I love you" but much harder to ensure that someone feels it. I've learned that love is not what we see in the movies—it is not grand gestures or gifts. I've learned that love cannot be forced or faked. I've learned that love is often a choice. And that this may not be the romantic fairytale that many of us want to hear, but it's the truth. Love is opening yourself up to another human's flaws and being courageous enough to show them yours. Love is safety and patience. Love is not only tolerating each other's differences but embracing and celebrating them. Love is giving someone the ability to be themselves. Love is fostering self-love in your partner and being conscious of their pain points. Love is remembering the little things they tell you and the big things they don't, but which are written all over their face.

The ache that comes after you walk away from someone who hurts you is not telling you that you were supposed to stay with them. It is you being reborn. It is the pain of revival. It is your body, heart, and mind grieving the life you thought you'd live and preparing for the life you are truly meant for. Losing the people that are wrong for us is still a loss that evokes agony in our hearts, regardless of how much we needed to lose them. We cannot welcome into our lives what is meant for us without first releasing what is not. And this ritual is not without pain. The next time you walk away from hurt and find yourself grieving, do not take this to mean you should have stayed. Take this as a sign that life is about to become full.

You can't make people love you. And while I know this might disappoint you and scare you and dishearten you, I believe that when you reflect on it further, it will free you. It will free you because it will loosen the hold that a false sense of control has over you. You won't have to feel like you need to be whatever it is that will prevent them from leaving. You won't have to wear a mask out of fear that if they saw the real you, they would leave. It is beyond liberating to say to the Universe, "bring me those that will love and welcome me into their lives and keep away those who won't." And I'm not saying that seeing them walk away won't cut deep and leave you with scars that will require some work to heal from, but I am saying that you won't have to grip people so tightly anymore. When you loosen your grip, you can let your hand and your heart rest.

It's not about whether they said they would love you forever. That's simply not enough. And that is just a promise, which can easily be broken. It's about the way they made you feel. And the way they didn't make you feel. It's about the doubts you had and the feelings you repressed. It's about you convincing yourself you were happy so that you wouldn't have to call those years a waste. It's about feeling like you were alone despite the fact that someone was lying next to you, living and breathing next to you and yet somehow not connecting with you. It's about all the times they shot down your hobbies, your soul callings, your worth. It's not about scraps of affection because anyone can dole those out at will. It's about not feeling like true partners, not feeling like they were a safe space, and not feeling like you recognized yourself with them. It's not about any of the things you used to think it was about.

I implore you to put down your lofty expectations that someone who has never come through for you suddenly will. I know you want to be an optimist and I applaud your faith. But here is a situation where blind optimism will only hurt you. I beg you to see things for what they are. And people for you they are. And yourself as someone who deserves so much more. I ask you kindly to learn from experience, let history guide you, and to not believe others to be what they simply can never be.

Amidst all the feelings I know you have—the regret and the sorrow, the shame and the grief—I hope there lies a tiny sliver of pride. Pride for finally walking away even though there were so many parts of you that didn't want to. Pride for the way you've held your head up and kept your eyes fixed on the future. A future where you know and do better, and don't let anyone use you again. Be proud of the way you keep getting up each morning, keep taking deep breaths, and keep pushing forward whether it's a good day, a hard day, or a day where you can't manage to feel anything at all. It is my wish for you that with time this feeling of pride only grows, more and more each day, until it outweighs all the others.

Some people are merely chapters in your book. You are not meant to read them over and over. You are not meant to get lost in them. Or live between their pages. They are part of your story, but they are not the entirety of your story. And though this truth may be hard to swallow, it will allow you to move through the remainder of the book with excitement. With hunger for the next chapter. With the ability to turn the pages of what comes next without so much sadness for what has passed.

While you are waiting to find the one, you can take on the role of the one for yourself. You can treat yourself kindly and speak softly to yourself. You can give yourself encouragement and soothing words when you fumble. You can laugh at your jokes and admire your beauty and take yourself out on dates. You can send yourself flowers and write yourself love notes, and sit and enjoy your favorite movie while drinking in your own delightful company. You can motivate, encourage, and inspire yourself. You can make a bucket list and promptly start crossing items off. You can make vows to yourself—to love yourself in sickness and in health. To be there for you. To always support your growth. You can make new friends and keep loving old ones and look at the beauty of the way your life is taking shape. Stop looking for the one and you might just see that you are the one.

I don't believe you should beg anyone to love you. You would never have to beg for love from the person truly meant for you. And if you do find yourself begging, what will you do on the days you don't have the strength or energy to beg? Those are the days you would need their unconditional love the most. If they are not in your life willingly then you really are alone anyway, even when they are beside you, aren't you? I don't believe you should convince anybody of your worth. I believe you should show them who you are through living your beauty daily and let those who see it, stay. There is no use in giving all of yourself to those who just can't see everything that you are.

Reclaim yourself. From the ones who hurt you. The ones who left you. The ones who think that just because they took pieces of you, that there is nothing good left. The ones who never saw your ability to regroup and regrow and head in a new direction. Reclaim yourself from anyone who made you feel like you need to plead for affection. Reclaim yourself from the version of you who didn't walk away earlier and the version of you who's scared you'll repeat those mistakes again. Reclaim yourself from anyone who doesn't believe you can rise and from anyone who seems to take pleasure in watching you fall. Reclaim yourself as many times as you need to in this life, over and over again until you're so sure of your ability to do so that you aren't even afraid of getting lost again because you know, you just know, you will be reclaimed.

We seem to think that at some point it's too late to find love, and this couldn't be further from the truth. Look at how many people, in all stages and ages of life, are just now finding love within themselves.

Other people cannot fix you. Other people cannot bear the responsibility of packing away your hurt and moving you towards a life where it is not the first thing on your mind each morning and the last thing on your mind each night. Other people cannot show you what you deserve–you decide yourself what you deserve. Other people cannot see into your mind, into your passions and fantasies and tell you how to convert them into reality. Other people cannot see how far you've come and envision exactly how far you are destined to go. Other people cannot convince you that you didn't deserve the hurt, and that you must walk away from those who caused it. You must realize yourself that you didn't deserve the hurt, and that you must walk away from those who caused it. Other people cannot lead you into healing. It is you who must decide where you'd like to go, stand up, put one foot in front of the other, and make your own way there.

This is how you grow.

Embrace change. Leave behind your past hurts, limiting beliefs, and self-doubt. Know that who you were yesterday does not have to be who you are tomorrow. Embrace the fact that you are allowed to change. Ignore those who shame you for changing. Work on yourself. Work on bettering your mindset, your circle, your daily habits. Question your "why." Question why you believed the ones who hurt you, why you've let others tell you who to be, and why you don't believe growth is a possibility. Don't be afraid to try new things. Have new experiences, make new friends, meet new parts of yourself. If you feel uncomfortable or like you are shifting internally, lean into it. Growth, by nature, can be uncomfortable. You are stretching the limits of who you thought you could be in order to step into a completely evolved you. Know that growth requires you to leave some people behind. It requires you to leave behind those who don't support you. Those who don't understand you. Those who want to keep you down. Growth requires you to leave behind the renditions of yourself that cannot go where you are meant to go.

If someone doesn't love you, it isn't you who misses out on an incredible love. It's them. You know what you have to offer. But you are allowing heartbreak to convince you that it isn't much. You know that you are magic. A spark. Brilliancy in the life of those around you. But you are grieving their loss as though you will never love again. You will. You just need to choose the right person to love again.

Things that are healing that may not feel like healing:
Taking the next breath. Continuing to picture your-
self happy, even if it seems unattainable. Reaching out
to a friend. Finding comfort in your own company.
Desiring healing. Desiring growth. Desiring content-
ment. Feeling a twinge of empathy for yourself. Pulling
yourself out of memories of the past. Daring to imag-
ine the future. Trying something new. Getting back
in touch with yourself. Being curious about who you
could be when you put down the pain. Sitting with the
pain. Sitting with the grief. Taking baby steps. Letting
yourself laugh when you don't want to. Feeling a flutter
of excitement in the morning. Not thinking about the
one who hurt you immediately upon waking. Exhaling.

It's not the pain that breaks you. It's your mistaken belief that it will never subside. It's your belief that you will live here, in this pain, forever. It's your thoughts that tell you, however incorrectly, that you deserve this pain. That it's all you'll ever know. That it's all others will ever see when they look at you. It's the way you cannot see past the pain and into a future where it's a distant memory. It's not the pain itself that feels so unbearable. It's the inability to understand how temporary it is. How fleeting it will be. How the heaviness weighing on your chest will lighten with time. How it will continue to lift, slowly but certainly, until you're not sure if it was ever there in the first place.

There is so much life after this season of hurt. There are so many good things to experience going forward. You won't be here in the pain forever, and you won't feel like this forever. There are cities to travel to. Friends to make. Countless books whose pages are just waiting for you to turn them. New people to explore the world with. New people to love. There are beautiful days filled with sunshine where you will wonder how you can feel so alive. There are rainy days where you will take comfort in a hot cup of tea and a poem that hugs you. There will be opportunities. Growth. Stillness. There is music you haven't danced to yet. There will be deep laughter you can't even imagine right now. Lazy days where you stay in bed and luxuriate in the quiet. And days full of adventure that will leave you breathless and exhilarated. There will be new levels of you to meet. Each extraordinary one waiting under a layer you need to strip back. Keep going. There is an abundance of life for you to live.

You will change. You will fall out of love with people you thought you'd love forever. And you will question friendships you've had your whole life. Your opinion on so many things will morph and transform as you gain more wisdom, experience, and life. You don't know everything, and you will never know everything. More than this though, you are *allowed* to change. Some people may try to make you feel bad for it. Because as you change, they have to change. They have to adjust their perception of who they thought you were and who they'd committed to believing you are. It doesn't mean you're at fault—it just means that this is uncomfortable for them. But the discomfort of others does not mean you should resist the change. You cannot keep yourself timid and scared, or you will never meet the you that's waiting at the end of this road. If you don't give in to who you are becoming, you will never become.

Healing is not a social media aesthetic. It's difficult and excruciating and it's turning a mirror towards your scars. It's so much more than showing your bubble bath setup and your glass of wine. It's a hell of a lot deeper than filming your morning routine in your aesthetically pleasing bedroom. It's facing your trauma and going to therapy. It's learning what to do with intrusive thoughts and memories you'd rather bury. It's ending friendships and relationships that don't support your growth and finding a new friend in a new version of yourself. It's nothing that can be neatly displayed in the little squares that grace our screens. It's finding a way to convince yourself to get up in the morning when you'd really rather not. And to close your teary eyes when you desperately need sleep. It's looking at everything in your life–every person, every practice, every thought–putting them all under a magnifying glass, and painstakingly weighing whether they help or hurt you. It's saying goodbye to the ones who do the latter. It's letting everything that you think is ugly about yourself come to the surface. In a world that values the beautiful, and often *only* the beautiful, I applaud you if you're on this journey.

Self-love scares people. They'll do anything to talk you out of it. They'll tell you it's selfish. It's distasteful. They'll tell you that it will leave you isolated and lonely. Self-love scares people because it's not easy to come by. It's found at the end of an often painful journey. Most of us don't even want to take the first step of that journey, let alone walk the whole path. So, they try to dissuade you from taking any steps at all. They don't want to face that part of themselves that is too scared to attempt it. They try to hold you back. Discourage you. Laugh at you. Just love yourself anyway. Love yourself for you and then step back and look at the people you attract into your life. When you master self-love, you won't stand for anything or anyone that will threaten it.

You need people who don't compromise your mental health. You need people around you who make your world that much brighter, that much sunnier, and a safer place for you to just be you. Whatever elements of you that is. Whether it's the you whose soul is content, or the you who has fallen and is trying to rise again. You need people who understand that you are more than one thing, and that all of it is beautiful. That you are a work in progress and this is a wonderful thing. You need people who support your growth, your desires, and your very presence. You need people who are not threatened by your self-love and who know that this doesn't make you selfish, this makes you *whole*. You need people who comprehend that you cannot give to them until you've given to yourself, and that to fault you for that would be denying you access to your own greatest resource.

You can build a magnificent life for yourself. No matter your situation, you can tidy up your life and make it just a little prettier and a little neater. And not the kind of pretty that's intended to impress or attract anyone, but the kind of pretty where it looks good from the inside because it *feels* good. You can plant flowers around you and you can plant flowers in the parts of you that have been hurt. You can start to clean up messes that were left behind by people who didn't care to stay and help. You can take the trash out, and be thankful that some of it probably took itself out already. You can hang paintings up on the walls, and you can return color to your own self. If you commit to doing this bit by bit, one day at a time, I promise your life will unfurl into something beautiful.

I spent so many years shrinking. Quitting. Abandoning myself. I listened to every person who said I can't. I hung on every word of those who looked down on me. I thought bravery and confidence just weren't for me. I believed the drops of attention, of affection, of so-called "love" were more than I even deserved. I thought saying yes to others when I desperately year-end to say no would earn me approval. Earn me love. Earn me something I was searching for but couldn't name. And now, it will take me time to unravel this. To examine it under a microscope, break down its parts, and understand why it was all so blatantly wrong. But I've started. I've started and now that I have, I can't go back. And nothing I've gone through has felt more like finally catching a glimpse of myself.

Do what you need to do today. Don't look so far down the line. Don't think about a week from now, a month from now, a year from now. When the pain is too heavy, just do what you need to do today. Take some breaths, and then take a few more. Put one foot in front of the other for as long as you feel you can. Understand that anyone who has ever healed has done so not all at once, but one day, one moment, one action at a time. Anyone who has ever healed started out in a place of intense pain. Anyone who has ever healed looks back and wonders how they made it through but is so incredibly grateful that they did.

When you try your hand at love again, it's not supposed to feel good. It's supposed to feel scary, daunting, and like you are learning to walk all over again. This is what it feels like to take a heart that has been annihilated and hold it out to the world once more. When you try your hand at love again, you are no longer bright-eyed and naïve. You have seen what others can do to your heart—the ease with which it can be crushed. But when you try your hand at love again, you also know how to handle the hearts of others. You know that there are many others out there who, just like you, are trying their hand at love again, too. You know how to hold these hearts with care. You know how precious they are and how in the wrong hands, they can be damaged. So you proceed with caution. And in doing so, you may find that somewhere out there is someone who will proceed with caution with your heart too.

Surrendering is different than giving up. Surrendering will release you. Surrendering is saying, "I don't know it all and I don't know where I'm going. But I have me by my side and that's all I need." Surrendering is finally acknowledging that you don't know better than fate, or the Universe, or whatever you want to call it. Surrendering is having the utmost trust that you will get to a fulfilling place where you accept what comes into your life and you accept what goes out of your life as part of the bigger plan. Surrendering is believing there is a bigger plan.

You will not find what is meant for you without losing some things. Some people, some thoughts, some habits. This is because the life meant for you is on the other side of all of that. Finding yourself is not always about creating something new. It's often about purging everything you have been letting weigh you down for so long. The people that drain you and the connections where you cannot be yourself. The self-defeating thoughts. The behaviors that keep you trapped. These are the things that are hiding you away from yourself and from the world. They're blocking your true vision of yourself and they're preventing you from shining. Let go. Lose the things that are not meant for you so you can usher in what is.

What language are you speaking to yourself in? Is it the language of softness and care? Or is the language of blame, shame, and anger? We get to choose how we speak to ourselves. We get to choose what narrative plays in our minds and which words we fill our heads with. In the same way that we long for others to speak kindly to us, we can make the choice to speak kindly to ourselves. The voice you hear inside of you is none other than your own and should be the most generous one you can muster. This world is filled with people who will speak harshly to us. There is no shortage of those who neglect to carefully choose the words they spew at you. Never let yourself be one of those people.

Say no. Say it often. Say it with your chest. Say no to anything that doesn't move you closer to a happy and healed version of yourself. Say no to people who don't think you deserve peace. Say no to yourself when you feel yourself slipping back into old patterns, old ways, old routines. Say no to those who expect you to put them first and you last. Say no to toxic people, toxic thoughts, toxic energy. Say no to memories that lie to you and tell you that you're stuck in the past. Say no to the parts of you that want to give up, the parts of you that don't think you're worthy, and the parts of you that don't believe in your own strength. Say no to anything that holds you back from your goals. To anything that tells you you're not good enough and you don't deserve to have standards. Say no to constantly saying yes to others. Say no to never saying yes to yourself.

This is how you heal.

Spend more time with people who let you be you, and less time with people who don't. Trust your own gut before you prioritize the opinion and advice of others. Journal. Get in touch with your own thoughts, feelings, and consciousness. Understand that some friendships are not meant to last. Wish them well and move forward in your own journey. Love fiercely but not at the expense of loving yourself. If you ever feel you must choose between a relationship and your own wellbeing, choose you. Hold out for the relationship that doesn't make you choose between the two. Find reasons to laugh, and bring laughter into the heart of those you love. Go to therapy. If you have something you're passionate about, chase it. Don't let fear of judgment or failure stop you. Say goodbye to those who hurt you. Both literally and figuratively. Believe that you are worth healing and deserve it wholly.

Learn to live your life unvalidated. Without needing unending approval from others on your decisions, your priorities, and your dreams. Learn to seek only your own validation so that you stay in harmony with your values. Trust yourself so deeply and so unwaveringly that you not only stop seeking the approval of everyone around you, but that you won't falter when you don't get it. Check in with yourself before big decisions the way you've grown so accustomed to checking in with everyone else. Use your intuition, rather than others, as your guide. Other people simply cannot lead you to the place you're meant for because they may not be on the road there themselves. So, if you want to have a chance at living the life that's for you, you've got to learn to live your life unvalidated.

It's when you let go of the idea that everything has to make sense. And you just start living, and breathing, and inhaling what is around you. It's when you start reveling in the beauty of walks, and fresh air on your skin, and the people in your life. It's when you realize the bliss that exists in delicious food and books and poetry and music. The bliss of snowfall outside with warm baths and soft blankets inside, while candles flicker against the walls of a quiet evening. It's when you sink into the pleasure of early nights and finding old love letters and flipping through photo albums. It's when you unexpectedly remember that one thing that made you laugh so hard all those years ago. It's when you fall into these things and let go of the idea that everything has to make sense. You learn that the seemingly trivial things are actually what you look forward to and you start to feel joy in your heart again. It's when you start to feel this joy just existing with yourself. And when you start to feel joy at the thought of just being with you, that's when it happens. That's when life starts to make sense.

Don't rush to fill the voids left behind by those who chose to exit your life. Don't rush to replace them with other people, vices, distractions, or self-pity. Let them sit for a while, open and quiet. Let them be a vacuum that might hurt at first, but which will naturally pull towards them something that is lighter and peaceful. If you leave them as is, eventually they will be restored with more of you. You will extend yourself into them and become a more whole and complete you. You will finally see how much of this world you really can and should take up.

Ask for what you need. Seriously, just do it. I know it sounds scary. I know it sounds like something that will push some people away. But you must ask for what you need. You are afraid that people may see you as needy, but we have to stop berating ourselves for simply having needs. Having needs doesn't make us hard to love. It makes us human. If you ask for what you need, one of two things will happen. Either they won't be able to deliver, and you'll finally know that they simply cannot be what you are searching for. This will hurt, but in the long run you will have the truth. Or, they will rise to meet your needs. And you will finally learn that you deserve all those things you need, but were always so afraid to ask for.

.

We tell ourselves that one day it will make sense and that one day we'll know why they had to leave, why we had to break, and why it had to hurt so damn bad. That someday the meaning, the message, and the lesson will be clear. But what if this weren't true? What if we never really come to a conclusion as to why it all had to come crashing down. Why they had to walk away. Why they had to unlove us. Why we had to sink to the bottom before we could even consider making our way back up. What if we just keep on living, breathing, reading, traveling to far-off places, making new friends, loving our families, getting lost in this life and collecting new experiences? What if we do this until we realize we aren't really that invested anymore in finding meaning in that sad thing that happened to us some time ago. What if over time it just becomes diluted and hazy and we conclude that it doesn't hold a lot of power over us anymore. It was, after all, nothing more than a sad thing that happened to us some time ago.

Never stop moving. Move towards your true self. Towards who you want to be, and who you know you really are. Move closer to the things that spark something bright in you. Move away from people who hurt you. Away from things that harm your core and threaten your safety. Don't stay in one spot. Don't stay in places that stifle you or ask you to detach from yourself. Don't stay with people who overpower you, demean you, or belittle you. Don't stay anywhere you feel suffocated. Make moves that excite you. Inspire you. Invigorate you. Whatever you do, just never stop moving.

Look at nature with awe. Look at the mountains and trees, and the rivers and wildflowers. Look at the clouds and the stars, and all the living beings we share this space with. And when you look at them, grasp how incredible and serendipitous it is that you are here to marvel at their beauty. Respect that whatever force is behind their existence is behind yours too. Understand that you make this world brighter in exactly the same way they do. Begin to look at yourself with the same awe and realize that if they have a place here, then you have a place here too.

You were never meant to be the same person forever. You were never meant to oblige the people who liked you the way you were before simply because it benefited them. Your entire being is dedicated to expansion and revolution. I cannot be certain of the purpose of life, but of this, I am certain: you are meant to change throughout it.

Your standards are not too high. The very fact that your standards exist makes them valid. The treatment you expect from the people in your life—from the people you allow into your life—can never be too much. If it's what you desire, it's simply not too much. Just because someone is unable to rise to meet your standards does not mean you have set them out of reach. It merely means that person is not for you. Not everyone will be for you, and this is okay. Instead of tolerating less than you wish for, acknowledge that you wouldn't have those desires placed on your heart if they weren't what you truly deserve.

Become who and what you want to be, and never stop becoming. Even if that means you periodically pivot. Even if that means your journey of discovery is never ending. Become what you always desired to be but were scared of due to the opinions of others. Become the form of yourself that feels the most authentic and the least forged. Become kinder to yourself, truer to yourself, closer to yourself. Become the type of person you'd like to be around and inspire others to become, too.

You deserve it all. You deserve the grace and the for-giveness. You deserve honesty from others, and honesty from yourself. You deserve someone who sees your flaws as reasons to love you. You deserve to see your own flaws as reasons to love you. You deserve kind-ness and patience and and contentment. You deserve time with yourself to cultivate yourself. You deserve to recognize everything you deserve.

Say goodbye to who you used to be. To the person you were before all the hurt. That was a you that endured mistreatment. Endured abuse. Endured so much pain you never deserved. That was a you who didn't know better. That person requires sympathy and generosity, but you do not need them to come back. You need to release that version of you just as much as you need to release the people who hurt you. You now get to be someone who carries memories of the old you within you, but who is so much wiser. So much stronger. So much closer to the *real* you.

I recall dancing so close to the edge of grief that I was certain I would fall. Plummet off the cliff and be lost forever. I couldn't decide if I was scared or invigorated. If I wanted to step back or step forward. I didn't know if I would feel terrified to fall, or relieved. On this cusp, in this pause between angst and healing, is where I discovered my choice. It's where I discovered my will and my faith. It's where I learned that the direction in which I step is determined by me. The direction in which I step will always be determined by me.

There are places I haven't traveled to yet, countries I long to see though I never have before. I yearn for places I have no history with and yet I know in my bones I want to experience them. I have an unwavering certainty that there are beautiful things waiting out there for me and that I am the beautiful thing waiting out here for what needs me. This is how I know I don't need to fear the unknown. This is how I know I will find happiness despite life taking me over here when I thought I wanted to go over there.

I don't thank myself enough. For carrying myself through this life. For being by my side even when I didn't want to be. I don't thank myself enough for making the tough calls to walk away from those who hurt me. And for holding myself when the ones who I thought would stay, didn't. I need to show more gratitude for my resiliency. The resiliency that I didn't really want but which was handed to me anyway. The gift that I opened and wanted to return at once. The gift that showed its worth way down the line, after years of heartache that only I was beside myself for. I'm learning to show gratitude for the way I've chosen to stay compassionate with myself when everyone around me was not. At the end of my life, I want to look myself in the eye and know that none of it went unnoticed. None of it was unappreciated. I wouldn't be where I am without everything I've given myself, and for that I deserve my thanks.

Sometimes simply surviving is success. Letting yourself exhale at the end of each day is, for some, no meaningless feat. The act of touching your feet to the floor each morning despite the heaviness in your chest, should not be discounted. You aren't always going to be in a place of thriving. Some of the pain can be so unrelenting that simply not succumbing to it feels like victory. If you have been holding up whatever is weighing you down, it's no surprise that your arms are tired. Realize that you wouldn't have been able to do so without immeasurable strength.

I am done yearning only for fire. For infatuation to be what I long for. I am ready for ease. For someone who makes me feel soft and strong at the same time. For someone I can fall into, instead of falling for. I want to feel like I can rest my head on them, and that my heart will be at rest too.

I cannot tell you which day you'll feel healed. I cannot tell you if it will be next week, in a month, in two years. Healing doesn't seem to work like this. It is not uniform and it does not treat everyone equally. What I can tell you, is that it can be yours. And that it will arrive in parts, rather than all at once. It will come. Maybe not as quickly as you wish that it would, but it will come.

You do not exist in seclusion. You need yourself, but you do not need only yourself. To experience the depth of love and connection is one of life's rarest gifts. On the route to self-love, we cannot forget to invite others along the way. When you are taught self-love, this is never to say that you should exist in isolation or love no other. The purpose of learning to love ourselves is not so that we love *only* ourselves. It is so that we love ourselves enough to choose the right people to love, and the right people to love us back. It is so that we share our love with those who truly deserve it and refrain from sharing it with those who leave us feeling less than. We learn self-love not to stay alone and keep others out, but so that we can let the true ones in.

The person you are today is fleeting. Think of all the journeys you have moved through to get here. Think about how you are constantly transforming. Growing. Shifting. Do not take the person you are today for granted. Do not miss the opportunity to get to know them. Sit with them now, before they are gone. This is the you that will deserve your gratitude in the future. When you get to the next you, it will become clear how they were shaped by the you that exists in the present.

The right one will want to see you grow. The right one will pray for your success. The right one will want your life to be a kaleidoscope of remarkable experiences. The right one will believe you are enough. The right one will look beyond your outer shell. The right one will not dim your shine. The right one will pray for your health. The right one will feel like home. The right one will be comfort. The right one will be safety. The right one will want to sit by your side and watch you unfold.

This is how you fall in love with yourself.

Pretend you are meeting yourself for the very first time. Note the uniqueness of your eyes, the way you stand, and your smile. View yourself through the lens of a lucky stranger who is catching their first glimpse of you. Realize that you are exactly the type of friend so many are searching for. Recall all the times you have been there for the ones you love. How you have lent loyalty, support, and a shoulder to cry on. Think about how much gratitude you have for those who have done the same for you, and then appreciate that someone out there is just as grateful for you. Remember yourself as a child. Think back to all the innocence that was inside of you and all the faith you had in yourself. Deep within you still lives that same innocent child who will forever deserve all of your love.

Sometimes what you think you've already grieved, comes back around again. What you think you've moved on from can plant itself firmly in front of you once more. Sometimes what you were so sure was far behind you, puts itself back in your path as though it never left. This doesn't mean you haven't made progress. It doesn't mean you haven't moved the needle towards healing. It just means that healing is not without interruption. Healing is a journey with many stops along the way.

When you meet the one—the one you choose, and the one who chooses you—do not forget how you walked yourself through the lonely moments. Do not disregard how you picked yourself up off the floor and convinced yourself to keep taking steps–one after another–just so you could keep moving forward towards something resembling peace. When you meet the one and your heart feels full, do not forget how you filled your own cup for all this time, and how you will continue to find wholeness within yourself. For the rest of your life, no matter who is next to you, you will still find wholeness within yourself. When you meet the one, do not consider them your other half. You are not half, and you never were. Delight in all that the one brings to you. Revel in the light they shine on you. But always remember that you are not half. And you never were.

The relationship that will have the biggest impact on your life is the one you have with yourself. You entered this world by your own side, you will move through it by your own side, and you will be by your own side until the end. Visualize the wonder your life could be if you nurtured this relationship, cared for it, watered it, and watched it bloom. Imagine the comfort you will feel if the person you are walking alongside for all your days is someone who is kind to you. Tender with you. A calming force towards you. Do not ever take this relationship for granted.

One day soon, you will realize that you are not a broken soul. You will not feel split in two forever. You will heal, flower, and rebuild. You will create something beautiful out of each season of heartache. You will feel whole again.

PARM K.C. is a Punjabi-Canadian writer from Alberta. She is a mental health advocate who has, from a young age, harnessed the therapeutic power of writing and poetry. She finds great fulfillment in offering comfort and empathy to others through her written words.

instagram.com/byparmkc
tiktok.com/@byparmkc